Resume

How To Write A Resume Which Will Get You Hired In 2016

Steve Gold

Introduction

A resume is the most important self-advertising tool at an individual's disposal when it comes to finding a job. Before you even get the opportunity to impress a hiring manager with your wonderful personality and people skills in an interview, your résumé will need to make a good first impression and stand up to the scrutiny of a perspective employer. Your resume acts as the key which will (or will not) unlock the door and grant you access to tout your qualifications and your suitability for a particular job position in person.

Due to the numerous methods available when it comes to advertising job openings in various channels today, it is easy for employers to get overwhelmed with more applications than they have the time to go through thoroughly. That means for every vacancy you apply for, you will most likely be competing against tens, hundreds, maybe even thousands of other job-seekers who share similar credentials, skills and experience to yourself.

With technology changing the way we live and work, there is no doubt job hunting is no longer the same as it was just a few years ago. Even so, writing a winning résumé will still make all the difference in getting you noticed by potential employers. This, in turn, will significantly increase your chances of getting a call back for an interview.

In this concise guide, you will learn about the "dos and don'ts" of great resume writing, and these tips and tricks are specifically geared towards finding a job in the present time. Even if you are an old hand at job hunting, you will also find helpful hints on how to tweak your resume so as to keep up with current trends.

With some modern additions to your resume, you can give yourself the competitive edge which may well be the all important deciding factor to whether or not you land that dream job!

Chapter 1

Job Hunting: Then vs. Now

It is an understatement to say that competition in the job market today is tougher than ever before. For the inexperienced job seeker, even the application process can be daunting, especially when one gets no reply or status update after sending out numerous applications.

For the experienced candidate looking for a career change, it can be confusing trying figure out how to get that all important advantage with recruiters. After all, of the many candidates competing for open positions, a tiny handful of hopefuls will get a call back for an interview, and most likely only one person will get hired in the end.

Significant shifts in hiring practices and job hunting can be attributed to an obvious source: technology. Specifically, the ubiquity of the internet and mobile technology in the 21st century is changing the way talent is discovered and recruited.

According to a late 2015 report – jointly produced by consulting firm, Boston Consulting Group, and research organization, Recruit Works Institute – the internet has become the primary channel for job searching. The report findings were gathered by surveying over 13,000 job seekers from 13 countries in order to establish a global view of the latest processes involved in searching for a job. It was revealed that approximately 55% of respondents sought new job opportunities online through job posting websites, compared to only 36% who consulted paper media and 33% who relied on referrals from friends and family.

However, the internet is breaking the recruitment mould in more than one way. While candidates and recruiters typically turn to job posting websites as a platform, social media and mobile applications are increasingly playing a pivotal role in people getting hired. This is hardly surprising, because we live in an era where people rely on social media and mobile devices to stay connected. Hence, several job search websites are already making headway by developing their own mobile apps, as an extension of their services, to make job postings accessible on handheld devices.

There is also a noticeable trend of employers turning to social media for recruitment, especially on professional network, LinkedIn. This is due in large part to the fact that a social media page gives a recruiter more insight into a candidate than just a resume accompanied by a cover letter.

Death of the Traditional Resume

With online job hunting and recruiting becoming the norm, the personnel in charge of hiring are getting bombarded with a larger than usual number of applications. TheLadders, an American-based company providing online job search services, found in a 2015 study that recruiters generally spend only six seconds reviewing each individual resume before deciding if the candidate is worth further consideration. That's assuming that your resume even gets reviewed by a human! Some companies, especially bigger corporations, employ automated tracking systems to screen through resumes. The same study also indicated that resumes which are deemed difficult to read at first glance, due to poor visual presentation, will be given even less time.

What this means for job seekers is that your resume has to be, not only professionally written, but also easy on the recruiters' eyes and mind in terms of it's visual presentation. It has to grab the hiring manager's attention from the moment it's viewed. Gone are the days where a neatly typed formal document on a white sheet will suffice. The modernized resume must equally showcase your individuality just as it touts your job qualifications.

So, when tailoring your resume for the next job you plan on applying for, it is worth remembering that you may only have six seconds to impress the person who's going to be receiving you resume. Make every word and visual element count!

In a nutshell, an outstanding resume in the modern age should meet the following criteria:

* Visually well presented for easy reading

* Eye-catching in design

* Written in a formal and professional manner

* Free of errors and spelling mistakes

* Contains words that "sell" you as a candidate (also known as "keywords" or "buzzwords")

* Relevant to the job being applied for

* Highlights a candidates qualifications in clear and concise sentences

* Makes it easy for the candidate to be contacted (email address, telephone number)

* Represents your individual professional brand

Take note of these key elements and keep them in mind when writing your resume. If you already have a written resume, run through the checklist above and see how it stacks up. Each of these points will be addressed in greater detail in subsequent chapters, and you will be guided on how to make each of them

work for you in your job applications.

Chapter 2

Anatomy of a Great Resume

A well-written resume is a document that gets you noticed and shortlisted from the tens and hundreds of candidates vying for a job position. It will be helpful to think of your job search process as building and selling your individual professional brand, with your resume being your main sales document.

People often associate certain values and image to brand names. Of course, you do not have to go to great lengths to 'brand' yourself as a company may brand a product. However, you know your own strengths, skills and expertise; think about what you can bring to an organization and how your resume can be made to reflect that.

In other words, your resume should give the impression that you are the right fit for an opening because you take pride in your work and you can add value to a team. You are not just another skilled person who is simply looking to make a living.

The following are 8 highly-important elements that an outstanding modern resume should incorporate in order to successfully convey your individual professional brand. These items are presented in their order of importance on a standard resume. While this format is not for everyone, it should be a good guideline to get you started. In chapter 3 we will cover the different types of resumes to accommodate the specific situations that job seekers may find themselves in. For now though, let's run through the "top 8" for a modern resume.

Make sure to take notes as you go along; by the end of this chapter, you should already be in a position where you are able to write the first draft of your new, improved and up-to-date resume.

1 - The bare basics: Name and contact information

The first and most important item on your resume is obviously your name, which should appear as the first item, in big bold font. Your phone number and email address should follow immediately after, as these are the fastest modes of communication for you to be reached.

2 - Location

A few years ago, the contact information on your resume would have included your mailing address. With the modern resume, a physical address is no longer necessary. There are two reasons for this.

Firstly, technology has sped up the hiring process meaning snail mail has almost no place in the process. Secondly, many companies are embracing the concept of the virtual workforce, using communication and collaborative tools to offer a remote working experience. That means a candidate's geographical location may be irrelevant in their getting hired. In addition, you risk identity theft if you include a full mailing address. Therefore, only put your city and state on your resume to indicate where you are based.

3 - Social media page

As a substitute for a mailing address, include the URL to your professional social media page. Companies are increasingly turning to social media for recruitment and screening, just as job seekers are heading there to look for opportunities. Social media has become a popular job search and recruitment platform because it allows candidates to showcase their extensive work history, while also allowing a recruiter to gauge a prospect's suitability. Moreover, social media is the most convenient means to get in touch and stay connected, even more so than emailing. Providing social media contact can also eliminate the need for another section in your resume; 'References'. In the not-so-distant past, references were people who could boost your credibility by testifying to your professionalism. When you direct a recruiter to your social media page, a reference will be just a few clicks and messages away.

A word of caution: make sure the social media address on your resume is dedicated to work only. LinkedIn is by far the most commonly used social media platform for professional networking. If you choose to include a Facebook or Twitter page, make sure said page is created for work and business purposes only. Do not put down your personal social media page!

4 - Professional summary

Traditionally, a resume would start off with what was known as the objective statement – a sentence that summarized your career goals. Times have changed, and hiring managers are more concerned with finding the right person for the job than what you are looking for. It is therefore safe to forego the objective statement and jump right into a synopsis of your skills, work experience, and accomplishments. Present the strongest points that will demonstrate why you are the perfect fit for the job, in a comprehensive, yet clearly and concisely written list or short passage. This section is meant to give an overview of what you are capable of, and a compelling summary can very well determine whether you are shortlisted or not.

To further capture the hiring manager's attention, instead of labeling this section 'Summary', use the header to highlight your area of expertise as it pertains to the job in question. For example, you can use the label 'Professional Writing Experience' if you are applying for the job as a staff writer, or 'Managerial Experience' if you are targeting a leadership position.

5 - Highlight your soft skills and talents, but not in a separate section.

Anyone can claim to have all sorts of soft skills and talents by listing them down on their resume. However, it's be more impressive to a potential employer – not to mention it will make your resume less cluttered – if you can demonstrate how you have applied these skills. Aim to weave your soft skills and talents into your work experience under 'Professional Summary', and throw in any achievements for good measure. This will give the recruiter a better idea of the specific value you could bring to their company. Here is a look at an example summary for the position of a project manager:

Forward-thinking professional who has developed and managed multimillion dollar, large-scale projects with a 90% project completion rate.

Self-motivated with more than 8 years of experience in managing multiple projects simultaneously, from the requirements gathering phase through to completion.

6 - Technical skills

A separate section listing your technical skills will be beneficial if you are applying for a skill-based job that requires specific qualifications, such as an IT specialist, medical technician or healthcare provider. Any special trade licenses or certifications that you hold also fall into this category (example: certified massage therapist and licensed forklift driver). Otherwise, this section can be omitted.

7 - Education and training

While a college degree remains essential, it is not always as important as skills learned from experience. This section of your resume should highlight any relevant formal education and training you've received. Keep it brief; if you have not attended any specialist studies or undergone any training, just put down the highest education received, which is normally the higher learning institute you attend. There is no need to write down your entire education history!

Additionally, if it is deemed relevant to the job you are applying for, you can use this section to show that you are dedicated to self-improvement on a continual basis. You can list any community college classes or online courses and workshops you have attended in order to build upon your skills. Make sure the additional training programs are recognized and hold credibility within the industry. There is little point in listing down one-time weekend hobby classes, which you took out of personal interest.

8 - Technological proficiency

In this day and age, it is safe to assume that you cannot get by without some degree of technological proficiency. Unlike the 'Technical Skills' section which is meant for specialized skills and qualifications, this last part of your resume is to let employers know that you are well-versed in using the technology required to do the job. List down software and programs which you are proficient in and use on a regular basis for the work you do.

Get Started!

Now that you know what goes into a modern resume, take action and get started on writing yours! If you already have one, update it according to these new guidelines. Once you have the "meat and beans" of your professional qualifications down, it is time to add the garnish by making your resume easy on the eye.

Chapter 3

Adding the Extra Touch

By now, you should have the first draft of your new resume. As mentioned already, the modern resume is not just a document packed with all of your required professional information. Before you can even get the recruiter to take the time and read about your qualifications, you need to first get them to give your resume a second look. To do so you'll have to make it stand out from among the hundreds they receive. Once you have all the relevant information written down, here are some ways you can add some impressive and attention-grabbing finishing touches to make your resume really stand out:

1 - **Visual presentation matters!**

Just as the clothes we wear play a part in creating the first impression we give to others, so must our resume. There is no quicker way to get your resume noticed than by livening up what would otherwise be a bland white sheet. Graphic designers and people in the creative arts field will have an advantage in this area, but even if you are looking for work in a corporate setting, it does not mean that you cannot add a little color to your job application to make it pop!

The key to successful visual presentation is to keep it simple and neat, so the reader's eyes are guided from the top to the bottom of the page. This can be accomplished by taking into account the following elements:

* **Font type.** Avoid getting too fancy, and stick to using a standard font that is easy to read. You can opt for a more decorative font for headers, but the rest of the resume – the body text – should be in a common font, such as Arial, Calibri, Georgia and Times New Roman. Whatever font you choose for the body text, make sure to keep it consistent throughout your resume and don't change it from passage to passage. You also want to keep you body text at a size that is easy to read and looks neat when

printed. The safest bet would is 10-14pt, depending on what font you use.

- **Formatting.** In visual terms, formatting refers to smart use of negative space in the overall layout, so that everything flows in a visually logical manner. This includes making decisions about spacing between lines of sentences, indentations, text alignments, margin sizes and headers. Adhering to proper and consistent formatting is crucial in making your resume look readable at a glance. Nothing is more off putting than the thought of having to read large blocks of small text crammed closely together. Remember: what is easy on the eyes is perceived as being easy on the mind.

Color. The modern resume is a colorful document that reflects and represents the candidate's individual brand. Use color to highlight and draw attention to important elements, such as your phone number and email, or section headers. While some color do spice a page up, take care that you do not overdo it or your resume will look messy. For a tip on proper use of color, look to some of the logos of world famous brands. How many colors are there to most logos? You will find that corporations and their logos tend to be associated with two to three colors. These are referred to as the corporate colors. As a rule of thumb, choose no more than three colors for your resume that you feel represent your professional brand, and stick to them.

2 - Do not underestimate the power of good written communication

Besides being a self-marketing document, your résumé is also a reflection of your written communication skills. For this reason, keep your language formal, professional and polite. Avoid witty plays on words and "cool" slang; you will come across as unprofessional and will not be taken seriously. Of course, it goes without saying that your résumé – and all your business correspondences for that matter – should be free of grammatical and typing errors. A single typo may nip your chances of employment in the bud, and you rarely ever get a second chance at making a good impression.

3 - Write with words that match

To manage the large influx of responses to hiring notices, many medium and large sized companies are using software to screen resumes and weed out candidates deemed unsuitable for the opening. This software searches for keywords, so your choice of words can make the difference between your application being accepted or rejected. This does not mean you have to pepper your resume with buzzwords in the hopes that the hiring personnel will search for them. Simply pay attention to the words used in the job posting and mirror this on your resume. For instance, if the job positing uses the term 'client relations', your resume may well get rejected if you wrote 'customer services' to describe your work experience.

4 - Make your resume web-friendly

Apart from in the case of a walk-in interview, you are most likely going to be presenting your resume in digital form. Hyperlink to your email address, social media page and portfolio website, so that you are just one click away, thus making things easy for a potential employer. It is also best to send your resume as a PDF file rather than a Word document, as the recipient cannot modify this type of document and it is easier for them to access. Given the large volume of applications hiring managers have to sort through, you would do yourself a service by making their job as easy as possible.

5 - Make every item relevant

One of the most common resume writing mistakes is to write down one's entire life history, from the elementary school you attended to your first part-time job, all the way to up to the present day. In actual fact, you only need to include information that can help convince the recruiter that you are the right candidate. A longer resume is not necessarily a better resume, and in reality, an overly long resume is likely to do more harm than good. Make every section, sentence and word count.

The Revision Checklist

Once you are done writing and spicing up your resume, the final step is to revise and polish it. Before you send it out, set your resume aside for a day or two so that you can return to it with a clear mind and fresh eyes. Run your resume by the checklist below to make sure everything is on point. Check it more than once, or get someone to help by proofreading your resume for you.

Content

- Is your contact information correct and properly highlighted so that it's easily noticeable at a quick glance?

- Have you included all the necessary info in a logical order?

- Does the description of your work experience illustrate how you successfully apply your soft skills to complete tasks?

- How does your resume show that you bring value to an employer?

- Are there grammar, spelling or vocabulary mistakes?

- Does you sentence structure make sense?

- Is every date and all other information correct?

- Is there irrelevant information that should be omitted?

- Is there relevant information not yet included?

- Do you incorporate the word choices used in the job posting?

- Are all your hyperlinks (for the digital copy to be sent via email) working properly?

Design & Formatting

- Do you have a uniform color scheme? (no more than 3 colors)

- Are all you line spacing between sections and body texts consistent?

- Are all your headers the same size?

- Are your margins and indents adequate to give the eyes enough "breathing room"?

- Does the page looked too crowded?

- Is the overall look of your resume neat?

- Is your choice of font easy to read?

Chapter 4

Tailor Fit Your Resume

In the world of employment, there is practically no substitute for skills demonstrated and acquired through work experience. Hence, it can be a confidence shaker if the professional summary part of your resume is not the largest section. The good news is there is no one-size-fits-all method for writing your resume. You can work around presenting your qualifications in a manner that accentuates your strengths while downplaying the areas you are lacking in.

The Chronological Resume

If you have been following the instructions closely thus far, you should have by now the complete modernized resume in the chronological format. This is considered the standard resume format and is most commonly used, characterized by listing previous employment experience in reverse chronological order, with relevant details presented as bullet-points.

The chronological resume allows you to show a consistent track record of employment. It also offers a recruiter insight into your upward career progression, the roles you have taken on and what you have accomplished. The drawback to this type of resume is that it makes employment gaps apparent. You may also be emphasizing employment history and titles over abilities and accomplishments. So, be sure to word your sentences in a way that it illustrates how your skills come into play when fulfilling previous roles.

The Functional Resume

What if you do not have extensive work experience? If your 'Professional Summary' section is too short, you may want to go with a functional resume format, where your skills take center stage to make your lack of experience less apparent. You can do this by placing the 'Technical Skills' and 'Education and Training' sections first, followed by your chronological professional summary.

A functional resume is suitable for fresh graduates who are just entering the work force, people who are changing careers, or those who have to temporarily leave the workforce due to personal circumstances. You can also opt for this format when applying for a skill-based position, where specialist training and certification are mandatory. The downside to a functional resume is that some experienced hiring managers will be able to see it for what it very well could be; a candidate's deliberate effort to obscure their work history.

You do not necessarily have to stick strictly to one type of resume format. In fact, you can write a hybrid resume that incorporates the best of both types.

One Page or Two Pages?

If you have an extensive work history, your resume may end up becoming too long for a single page. In such a case, it is acceptable to make a two-page resume, but no more than that.

When you resume is longer, you want to make sure that you do not compromise visual presentation by making the document too wordy and cluttered. List only your most recent 10 years of work, or write about the last three to five jobs you have held in detail. Add an additional 'Prior Professional Experience' section where you list all previous employment, including the dates of employment, but without the bullet list describing your roles.

Be reminded that you do not have to list your entire work history from the time you left school. Only add the 'Prior Professional Experience' section if you have decades' worth of relevant experience leading up to the present.

All Experience is Good Experience

Ultimately, regardless of the format you choose or the length of your resume, recruiters are mainly concerned with what you can offer an organization in terms of skills and expertise. The key is to demonstrate, through your resume, how you acquired and were able to apply the skills an employer needs. Ideally, you want to show that you have gained skills through work experience. If that cannot be done, you can buff up your resume by listing activities that enable you to gain the relevant skills required for the job.

For instance, a fresh graduate with limited professional experience can add any volunteer work, extracurricular activities, vocational training, or internship they have done to their resume. Consider this example: A budding journalist applying for an entry level job at a sports publication would stand a better chance if athletic achievements were noted on their resume, compared to a candidate with the same academic credentials. The experience is relevant because the recruiter may take it as an indication that the candidate is passionate about the industry, is likely to take the job seriously, and could bring in knowledge of sports that other candidates do not have.

The takeaway here is if it makes you look good in the eyes of a recruiter, it should be on your resume!

Use a Multimedia Approach

If you are up for going the extra mile to make up for a lack of experience to show on your resume, consider making a video where you introduce yourself and talk about how your abilities make you the right fit for the job. Dress professionally (like you would if you are attending a job interview), shoot your video with a good camera, under good lighting, and upload it to your social media page. Then, add a hyperlink to your video to your resume.

Resumes with video accompaniment are gaining popularity, especially in creative and media industries. It gives the recruiter a chance to see you speak without having to call you in for an interview first.

The Next Step

Is your resume showcasing your abilities or is it giving away your amateur job hunter status? How else can you fine-tune your resume to perfection?

Look through your resume again with a critical eye this time. If you are a recruiter, would you hire *you*? Try to have someone who is more experienced in the field you are hoping to enter read through your resume, and see what feedback they have to offer.

Next, we'll look at resume mistakes to steer clear of.

Chapter 5

Resume Writing Pitfalls

There are essentially two parts to the job application process. First, you have to convince a hiring manager, on paper, why you should be considered. If you're successful in this first step, you will get a chance to further convince an employer that you are the one for the job when invited to take a telephone interview or a face-to-face interview.

A great resume fulfills the requirements of the first part of the hiring process. The purpose of a resume is to obtain an interview, not a job. If you are down on your luck with job hunting and have been sending out copies of your resume for a while without any callbacks, you could possibly be committing the following resume sins. Take another critical look at your resume and make sure you have covered your bases before sending it out again. Some of these pitfalls not only pertain to your resume, but also to your overall job search strategy.

Not staying current.

There is no room at all for complacency in the ever-competitive job market. We live in an ever-changing world and if you're not keeping up with changes, that means you're falling behind. Are you still using the same old resume you used a few years ago? If so, time to update it for the digital age.

Updating your resume should be something you do constantly. This does not only mean adding new details to your job search document; it also means keeping your skill set current by staying up to date with trends and learning everything you can about your industry. Employers tend not to be impressed by unemployed candidates who slack in their job searching efforts, so if you are currently unemployed, take the initiative to acquire or upgrade your skills through volunteer work and extracurricular activities – things which you can add to your resume and talk about in a job interview. If you are in a creative field, keep your portfolio up-to-date and add new examples even during periods of unemployment. After all, you will not have anything new to add on to your resume if you are not actively improving yourself in preparation for the next job opportunity.

2 - Being generic

One of the quickest ways to have your resume end up in the reject pile is to write only one generic resume and send it out to every job that piques your interest, hoping for a lucky break. This approach to job hunting is counter-productive. It's not hard for a recruiter to spot a candidate who does not put effort into their application; the first telltale sign is a lengthy resume that packs in the candidate's entire life history, regardless of whether those credentials are pertinent to the job in question. If the company uses an applicant tracking system, you will lessen your chances even further through leaving out the important industry-specific or job-specific keywords.

A solution to this practice is to first be selective of the jobs you choose to apply for; narrow down your targets to a handful which your skills and experience are best suited to, and then tailor your resume to cater specifically to those jobs.

3 - Under or overdoing it with the design

A little color and creative use of space can get your resume noticed. However, focusing too much on design, or worse, over decorating the document, without giving enough attention to the contents can work against you. Likewise, complete disregard for the most basic formatting can also make your resume unreadable. Remember: you have a six-second test to past. Strike a balance between design and content!

4 - Using first person pronouns or writing in the third person

Your resume should be written in the first person, with all first person pronouns omitted. That means no 'I', 'me' or 'my'. Keep in mind that even with the pronouns omitted, your sentences are still representative of your voice. So, be careful that you also do not make the mistake of writing in the third person. A correct sentence example would be. "Brainstorm ideas and develop products", not "Brainstorms ideas and develops products."

A tip to formulate correct statements in the first person is to imagine you are talking directly to the hiring manager. Conversely, you can test out if your sentence structure is properly written by checking to see if they are still correct if first person pronouns are added in.

5 - Not proofreading

No matter how qualified you believe yourself to be, poor sentence structure, improper use of words and grammar, along with spelling mistakes and typing errors are all highly likely to ruin your chances of being invited in for an interview, let alone of securing a job. Errors in the resume give the impression of unprofessionalism and lack of effort, so proofread your resume more than once before sending it out. If you feel that language is not one of your strong points, enlist the help of someone else to revise your document.

Also, be sure to check that your contact information is correct. Otherwise, do not be surprised why you have not gotten a call or email from any prospective employers!

6 - Being a copycat

One of the reasons people make mistakes when it comes to the language they use in their resume is because they copy the exact wording from their company job description. These mistakes are always easy to spot because job descriptions are usually written in the third person and tend to be full of jargon. Your resume is not a description of jobs you have held in the past. It is a marketing tool that should sell your abilities. Besides, if you are copying word for word from the job manual of a company you have previously worked in, it is, strictly speaking, a form of plagiarism.

With this in mind, copying the design and layout of an existing resume or of a sample resume floating around the internet is just as bad. If you are not sure where to start in regard to the design aspect, use a generic template as a guideline, but be sure to modify it as much as necessary in order to make it suit your needs.

7 - Not having an online presence

Having an up to date professional social media account shows that you are invested in your career and are passionate about the industry which you are in. If you want to take it one step further, you can start a blog about your industry. You online presence can be a handy extension of your resume, and it can be highly advantageous for the modern resume to contain a link to some sort of professional network or outlet. Just make sure you stay active and keep it updated!

8 - Not separating work and play online

What could be worse than not having a social media link on your resume? Putting down a personal account! It is acceptable to use more common social networks like Facebook and Twitter for your job search, especially for candidates in a creative industry, but create a separate professional account for this purpose. Make sure to also keep the contents of this account strictly professional and work related. The recruiter does not need to know what you do in your private life.

9 - Treating your resume like a biography

One of the biggest pet peeves among recruiters is overly long resumes, with large blocks of text that attempts to be narrative. It can not be emphasized enough that your resume does not need to include every job you have ever worked in or every training course you have attended. It certainly does not need to contain unnecessary background information. Statements like, "Assisted in the development of marketing material in father's company" is completely pointless. Adding personal information like age, marital status, height and weight is even worse, and will almost certainly get your application tossed aside.

As a rule of thumb, list only details of jobs you have held in the past 10 years, and non-work achievements (such as receiving an award or scholarship) that are no older than three years, unless they are extremely impressive.

10 - Not emphasizing the right strengths, achievements and results

Quite possibly the most common error made when it comes to resume writing is focusing on work duties in your professional summary without mentioning measurable results. A prospective employer is not simply interested in what you did; they want to know how well you did it, so that they have an idea of what you will be able to bring to the company if hired.

Giving generic job descriptions for past positions does not argue your case effectively as to why you should be hired. Instead, be sure to place emphasis on the contributions you have made in past jobs. Whenever possible, describe a soft skill employed in the process and include numbers to quantify your results. A statement that says, "Diligently and consistently analyzed market trends that contributed toward a 30% growth in sales," is much more impactful than saying, "Analyzed market trends for the sales team."

The professional summary is the protein of your resume, and thus deserves extra attention. If you are unsure how to make your achievements stand out, consider the following questions:

* What did you do to improve the current processes in your previous work place?

* What problems did you solve?

- Is the success you achieved measurable via concrete facts and figures?

- Did you perform your responsibilities better than other colleagues?

- How can your performance be measured?

- What have you done that your previous boss would be proud of you for?

- Did you help to solve any problems that could have helped your former organization say that you were a valuable asset to the company?

- How could you show the results of your efforts? (again, look to the facts and figures)

- Have you won any prizes or awards of excellence, or contributed to your former company winning any awards?

Conclusion

As you have no doubt see, there are many factors involved when it comes to writing the perfect resume, and things are perhaps not as simple now as they may have been in the past. However, by following the guidelines outlined in this book, you will be well on your way to securing an interview and one step closer to your dream job!

Good luck!

A message from the author, Steve Gold

Thank you for your purchase of this book. Finally, if you enjoyed this book, **please** take the time to share your thoughts and post a review on Amazon. It will only take a couple of minutes and I'd be extremely grateful for your support.

Thank you again for your support.

Steve Gold

FREE BONUS NUMBER !

As a free bonus, I've included a preview of one of my other best-selling books, "Warren Buffett - The Business & Life Lessons Of An Investment Genius, Magnate & Philanthropist"! Scroll to the end of this book to read it.

ALSO...

Be sure to check out my other books. Scroll to the back of this book for a list of other books written by me along with download links!

FREE BONUS!: Preview Of

"Warren Buffett - The

Business & Life Lessons Of

An Investment Genius,

Magnate & Philanthropist"!

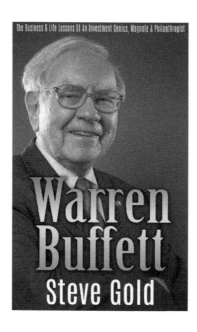

If you enjoyed this book, I have a little bonus for you; a preview of one of my other books "Warren Buffett - The Business & Life Lessons Of An Investment Genius, Magnate & Philanthropist". In this book, I take a closer look at exactly who Warren Buffett is as well as examining the truly extraordinary accomplishments he has managed to achieve in his life thus far. In the book I dig deeper into 7 of the major principles that have helped Buffett achieve such unbelievable success. Enjoy the free sample, and feel free to click on the purchase link below if you would like to learn more about this truly incredible individual!

Introduction

It may be a bold statement, but I believe that no one in the world of investment who's alive today understands success, wealth and, perhaps even happiness, the way that Warren Buffet does. Not only does the so-called "Sage of Omaha" know how to generate an immense fortune, he also has a solid comprehension of how finite and impermanent money actually is. He may have made a name for himself as an investment strategist, but Buffet often speaks of how loose and overrated the link between wealth and quality of life can be. He would even go as far as to stress – somewhat paradoxically – that the more money one has, the less free and unhappy one is likely to become.

Indeed, it can almost seem at times that despite his influential career in finance, Buffett does not place great importance on money and material possessions. His net worth may be up in the billions, but he lives in the least billionaire-like fashion. Buffett, who's the antithesis of the typical image of a wealthy business magnate, owns a considerably modest amount of tangible assets compared to his nine-figure net worth peers, and he appears to be disinterested in the extravagant lifestyle of the rich and famous. He embraces the simplicity of daily life, reminding himself from the onset of his career that there are no greater assets one can possess than good health, as well as remembering that the key to happiness lies in the priceless bonds one creates with friends and family.

His impartiality to wealth could not be more evident than in his numerous philanthropic efforts, which includes record-breaking donations amounting to more than half of his accumulated wealth over time.

Regardless of where one stands in life and whatever one's aspirations are, plenty can be learned by examining the core values that made Warren Buffett one of the most successful and wealthy individuals in the world.

In the chapters that follow, you will see that business and personal success is not so much a result of strategic investment decisions, but rather that it results from cultivating a number of personality traits essential for navigating the world of commerce.

Additionally, as Buffett has continuously demonstrated, good character and adherence to moral principles goes a long way in ensuring long-term success, wealth and happiness.

Warren Buffet has made great contributions to the world in the form of a long-standing investment track-record along with his enormously generous philanthropic endeavors. As a business and investment magnate, Buffett's approach to growing and managing wealth contains a certain humility that is so rarely given attention in a field that is predominantly about strategies and figures. Drawing from his own life experiences, Buffett acknowledges the human element that is often overlooked when it comes to accumulating and maintaining wealth. His philosophy and principles are simple, yet so powerful that they go beyond investment portfolios and apply to practically every aspect of our lives.

Buffett's extensive career achievements, however, can never measure up to the impressive life he has led. Living by his beliefs and principles, he proves that with patience, perseverance, diligence and hard work, one can build a financially stable and fulfilling life. Most importantly, he has exemplifies that a quality life is one which is lived with generosity, integrity and modesty.

Chapter 1

Plan For The Future

"Someone's sitting in the shade today because someone planted a tree a long time ago."

Warren Buffett

The path to financial and personal success is not lined with gold but with golden values.

Keeping your path straight, free from distractions or temptations, is the best vision anybody can take while planning their financial future. Investment strategists such as Warren Buffett suggest instilling in yourself from a young age the ability to stick with your plan following concrete steps to get to where you want to be.

Buffett had a vision from when he was a child that he would be rich by investing his money in himself instead of giving away his hard earned money to somebody else. That vision started when he was a young boy in Washington, D.C., where his father served four terms in the U.S. House of Representatives after moving the family from Omaha, Neb. His father was originally a stockbroker and Warren learned the trade of investing by being close to his father. As a teenager in D.C., Buffett invested in placing pinball machines in barbershops. He took the money from those pinball machines and invested in more machines.

He was fortunate from the beginning to have a father who stressed the importance of making sound financial decisions to improve his future. Every bit of his money was important to his development in becoming the second wealthiest person in America, behind business magnate Bill Gates.

Buffett, who was born on Aug. 30, 1930, stresses to young people today to grasp what they have and build on it before giving it away to credit card companies. He warns against spending sprees and living outlandishly. His message: Everything has a price and what you spend today will affect your savings for tomorrow, not only for yourself but for your children and grandchildren.

"Money doesn't create man, but it is the man who created money," Buffett said in a recent interview with CNBC.

Money does not define Buffett although he is worth billions. He has maintained his humble values from his modest upbringing in Omaha. He continues to live in the same home in Omaha that he bought in 1958 for $31,500. The 6,000-square foot home in the Dundee-Happy Hollow Historic is valued today at

$250,000, still a modest price for the mega-billionaire who is nicknamed the "Oracle of Omaha".

It is the only house Buffett owns, which is another rarity for a billionaire who has more personal wealth than some third-world countries. He once also owned real estate in Laguna Beach, Calif., but sold that property in 2005 for $5.45 million, a profit of more than $4 million from when he purchased it in 1993 as a vacation spot for him and his wife. Even when he tried to live lavishly, he made a profit from it, although this was an isolated case where he strayed from his basic principles.

Buffett always had a clear vision of his future since his childhood. He became an investor when he was 11. In his high school yearbook, he described himself as a "future stockbroker" although he was well on his way. From the start, he had the confidence to achieve his goals because he knew his path would be free of distractions or temptations. He was never consumed by excess to a fault.

"I don't think standard of living equates with cost of living beyond a certain point," Buffett said about his modest home during a 2014 shareholder meeting for Berkshire Hathaway, an American multinational conglomerate holding company that he owns. "Good housing, good health, good food, good transport. There's a point you start getting inverse correlation between wealth and quality of life. My life couldn't be happier. In fact, it'd be worse if I had six or eight houses. So, I have everything I need to have, and I don't need any more because it doesn't make a difference after a point."

Buffett is on record saying that having more wealth actually reduces the quality of life. In his opinion, the quality of life is based on basic needs. That includes having good health, adequate housing, nourishment and transportation. Not all who are afforded these needs are content or satisfied. People crave bigger homes, souped-up cars and meals at expensive restaurants. Many of us believe happiness comes from having an extravagant lifestyle.

Buffett's clear vision of his future from the time he was raised in Omaha and Washington, D.C., has allowed him to become wealthier than even the greediest person can imagine. The invaluable plans from when Buffett was young that created his happy existence involved taking an inventory of his life, embracing the simplicity of his life and never straying from his core values.

When taking an inventory of his life during his formative years at the University of Nebraska and Columbia Business School, Buffett realized his greatest asset aside from his health was his association with his significant other, family and long-standing friends. His inherent assets – his personality, humor and education -- all played a part in his fruitful association with others. They carry no price tag. Those assets define him more than money ever will.

Buffett's simple pleasures of life include keeping to himself, reading a book without interruption. His idea of a pleasurable evening since his high school years is not being out on the town but instead staying home to watch television and enjoy a hot cup of tea. Buffett believes that taking every opportunity to embrace your simple pleasures is the most valuable move you can make for your future.

Throughout the years, Buffett has stayed true to his core principles and values. He never takes a chance with his investments. He sticks with investing in the sectors he believes will produce the most profit. Maintaining a clear vision of the values needed to reach prosperity has allowed Buffett to stay atop the business world, never wavering.

Check out the rest of "Warren Buffett -
The Business & Life Lessons Of An
Investment Genius, Magnate &
Philanthropist" on Amazon.

Check Out My Other Books!

Elon Musk - The Biography Of A Modern Day Renaissance Man

Elon Musk - The Business & Life Lessons Of A Modern Day Renaissance Man

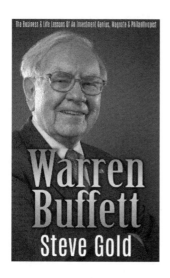

Warren Buffett - The Business And Life Lessons Of An Investment Genius, Magnate And Philanthropist

Steve Jobs - The Biography & Lessons Of The Mastermind Behind Apple

Management - Achieve Management Excellence & World Class Leadership Skills In 7 Simple Steps

Sales - Easily Sell Anything To Anyone & Achieve Sales Excellence In 7 Simple Steps

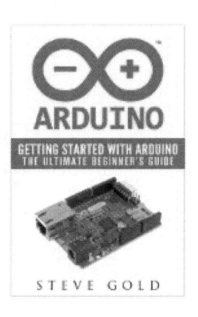

Arduino - Getting Started With Arduino: The Ultimate Beginner's Guide

(If the links do not work, for whatever reason, you can simply search for these titles on the Amazon to find them. All books available as ebooks or printed books)

Made in the USA
Lexington, KY
25 November 2016